PLANT BASED
DIET
COOKBOOK

FOR BEGINNERS

SARA GREGER

DISCLAIMER

The information contained in the Book is for informational purposes only, and in no way constitutes the making of a diagnosis or prescription for treatment.
The information contained in this book is not intended and should not in any way replace the direct relationship doctor-patient or specialist examination.
It is recommended that you always seek the advice of your physician and/ or specialists for any reported indication.

CONTENTS

CONTENTS

Farro Soup

Prep Time: 5 min   **Cooking Time:** 20 min   **Servings:** 6

Ingredients:

- 3 tablespoons extra-virgin olive oil
- 2 celery ribs, chopped
- 2 medium carrots, chopped
- 3 medium shallots, chopped
- 3 garlic cloves, minced
- 1 cup farro
- 6 cups vegetable broth, homemade or store-bought, or water
- 1 (14.5-ounce) can diced tomatoes, undrained
- 2 bay leaves
- 1 teaspoon salt
- ½ teaspoon freshly ground black pepper
- 3 cups cooked or 2 (15.5-ounce) cans cannellini or other white beans, drained and rinsed
- ¼ cup chopped flat-leaf parsley

Directions:

1. In a large saucepan, heat 2 tablespoons of oil over medium heat. Add the celery, carrots, shallots and garlic. Cover and cook, stirring occasionally for 5 minutes.

2. Add the spelled to the pot along with the broth, tomatoes, bay leaves, salt and pepper. Bring to a boil, then lower the heat and cook, uncovered, until the vegetables and spelled are tender for about 1 hour.

3. Finish and serve

4. Add the beans and parsley, then simmer for 20 minutes, adding more broth if the soup gets too thick. Remove and discard the bay leaves before serving.

5. Ladle in the bowls. Drizzle with the remaining 1 tablespoon of oil, then serve

Mediterranean Vegetable Soup

Prep Time: 5 min   **Cooking Time:** 45 min   **Servings:** 4

Ingredients:

- 1 tablespoon extra-virgin olive oil
- 1 medium yellow onion, chopped
- 1 medium carrot, chopped
- 3 garlic cloves, minced
- 1 medium red bell pepper, cut into ½-inch dice
- 1 medium fennel bulb, quartered and cut into ¼-inch slices
- 1 medium zucchini, chopped
- 1 (14.5-ounce) can diced tomatoes, undrained
- 1 cup vegetable broth
- Freshly ground black pepper
- 8 ounces white or porcini mushrooms, lightly rinsed, patted dry, and sliced
- 3 cups fresh baby spinach
- 1½ cups cooked or 1 (15.5-ounce) can cannellini beans, drained and rinsed
- ½ teaspoon dried basil
- ½ teaspoon dried marjoram
- 2 tablespoons minced fresh parsley

Directions:

1. In a large saucepan, heat the oil over medium heat. Add the onion, carrot, garlic and pepper. Cover and cook until softened for 7 minutes.

2. Add the fennel, courgettes, tomatoes and broth. Bring to a boil, then reduce the heat to low. Season with salt and black pepper, cover and simmer until vegetables are tender for about 30 minutes.

3. Finish and serve

4. Incorporate the mushrooms, spinach, beans, basil, marjoram and parsley. Taste and adjust toppings as needed. Simmer for another 10 minutes. Serve immediately.

Lentil Soup

Prep Time: 10 min   **Cooking Time:** 20 min   **Servings:** 3

Ingredients:

- 1 teaspoon extra-virgin olive oil
- 2 carrots, peeled and chopped
- 1 onion, diced
- 2 garlic cloves, minced
- 1 tablespoon dried herbs
- 1 to 2 tablespoons apple cider vinegar
- 5 cups water or Vegetable Broth
- 1 cup dried split red lentils
- ¼ teaspoon salt
- 2 tablespoons nutritional yeast (optional)

Directions:

1. Heat the extra virgin olive oil in a large saucepan over medium heat.

2. Add the carrots, onion and garlic and sauté for about 5 minutes, until the vegetables have softened.

3. Add the dried aromatic herbs and vinegar, let it sizzle and blend the bottom of the pan. Mix the water and the lentils. Bring the soup to a boil, then reduce the heat to low. Simmer for about 15 minutes, until the lentils are very soft and creamy. Incorporate the salt and nutritional yeast (if used).

4. Finish and serve

5. Using a hand blender, blend the soup until smooth or allow it to cool slightly before transferring it to a counter-top blender to puree. Leftovers can be stored in an airtight container for up to 1 week in the refrigerator or up to 1 month in the freezer.

6. Per Serving (about 2 cups) Calories: 457; Protein: 31g; Total fat: 5g; Saturated fat: 1g; Carbohydrates: 76g; Fiber: 16g

Four-Bean Chili

Prep Time: 10 min   **Cooking Time:** 15 min   **Servings:** 6

Ingredients:

- 2 tablespoons extra-virgin olive oil
- 1 onion, chopped
- 4 garlic cloves, minced
- one 15-ounce can black beans, drained and rinsed
- one 15-ounce can kidney beans, drained and rinsed
- one 15-ounce can pinto beans, drained and rinsed
- one 15-ounce can white beans, drained and rinsed
- two 15-ounce cans ro-tel roasted tomatoes and peppers
- 2 cups vegetable stock
- 3 tablespoons chili powder
- 1 teaspoon sea salt

Directions:

1. In a large saucepan, heat the extra virgin olive oil over medium-high heat until it glows.

2. Add the onion and cook until softened for about 5 minutes. Add the garlic and cook until fragrant for about 30 seconds. Add the beans, tomatoes, peppers, vegetable stock, chili powder and salt.

3. Finish and serve

4. Cook, stirring occasionally until heated through, for about 10 minutes. Serve immediately.

Potato and Corn Chowder

Prep Time: 5 min   **Cooking Time:** 16 min   **Servings:** 6

Ingredients:

- 1 tablespoon olive oil
- 2 medium carrots, peeled, chopped
- 2 ribs celery, chopped
- 1 medium white onion, peeled, chopped
- 1 ½ teaspoon minced garlic
- 1/4 cup all-purpose flour
- 1 teaspoon dried thyme
- 4 cups chopped white potatoes
- 2 cups vegetable broth
- 2 cups almond milk, unsweetened
- 3 tablespoons nutritional yeast
- 1 cup frozen corn kernels
- 1 teaspoon salt
- 1/4 teaspoon ground black pepper

Directions:

1. Take a large pot, put it on medium-high heat, add the oil and when it is hot, add the onion, carrots, celery and garlic and cook for 5 minutes until golden brown.

2. Then sprinkle with flour and thyme, mix until coated, cook for 1 minute until flour is golden, then add yeast, potatoes, milk and broth and mix until blended.

3. Bring the mixture to a simmer, cook for 8 minutes until tender, then add the corn and season the soup with salt and black pepper.

4. Serve immediately.

Nutrition:
Calories: 126 Cal Fat: 3 g Carbs: 18 g Protein: 6 g Fiber: 3 g

Cauliflower Soup

Prep Time: 10 min   **Cooking Time:** 60 min   **Servings:** 4

Ingredients:

- 1 medium head of cauliflower, cut into florets
- 1 small white onion, peeled, diced
- 1 medium carrot, peeled, diced
- 1 stalk of celery, diced
- 1 head of garlic, top off
- 2/3 teaspoon salt
- 1/3 teaspoon ground black pepper
- 1 teaspoon smoked paprika
- 2 tablespoons nutritional yeast
- 1 teaspoon hot smoked paprika
- 4 tablespoons olive oil
- 12 ounces coconut milk, unsweetened
- 4 cups vegetable broth
- ½ cup chopped parsley

Directions:

1. Turn on the oven, then set it to 400 degrees F and let it preheat.
2. Place the top of the garlic on a sheet of aluminum foil, drizzle with 1 tablespoon of oil and then wrap.
3. Put the cauliflower florets in a bowl, drizzle with 2 tablespoons of oil, season with salt and black pepper and mix until well coated.
4. Take a baking sheet, spread the cauliflower flowers in a single layer, add the wrapped garlic and cook for 30 minutes until roasted.
5. Then place a large saucepan over medium-high heat, add the remaining oil and when hot, add the onions and cook for 3 minutes.
6. Then add the celery and carrot, continue cooking for 3 minutes, season with salt and paprika, pour in the broth and bring to the boil.
7. Add the garlic and roasted florets, bring the mixture to a boil, then bring the heat to medium-low and simmer for 15 minutes.
8. Blend the soup using a hand blender, stir in the milk and yeast until they blend and simmer for 3 minutes until hot.
9. Garnish the soup with parsley and then serve.

Nutrition:

Calories: 102.2 Cal Fat: 6.3 g Carbs: 11 g Protein: 2.7 g Fiber: 4.6 g

Matzo Balls

Prep Time: 15 min   **Cooking Time:** 0 min   **Servings:** 12

Ingredients:

- 1 cup matzo meal
- ½ teaspoon onion powder
- ½ teaspoon salt
- ¼ teaspoon freshly ground black pepper
- 1 cup crumbled drained firm tofu
- 1/3 cup vegetable broth, homemade or store-bought, or water
- 2 tablespoons fresh minced dillweed
- 2 tablespoons chopped fresh parsley
- ¼ cup extra-virgin olive oil

Directions:

1. In a medium bowl, combine the matzo flour, onion powder, salt, and pepper. To put aside.

2. In a food processor, combine the tofu, stock, dill, parsley, oil, and puree. Stir the tofu mixture into the matzo mixture and mix well. Cover the bowl and refrigerate it for 1 hour or overnight.

3. Bake

4. Preheat the oven to 375 ° F. Lightly grease a baking sheet and set aside. Divide the matzo mixture into 12 equal portions. Use your hands to form very compact balls and arrange them on the oiled baking sheet. Cover well with aluminum foil and bake for about 30 minutes.

5. Finish and serve

6. Set aside to cool. Serve hot.

Vegetable Stew

Prep Time: 5 min   **Cooking Time:** 55 min   **Servings:** 4-6

Ingredients:

- 2 tablespoons canola or grapeseed oil
- 1 yellow onion, chopped
- 3 garlic cloves, minced
- 1 or 2 fresh hot chiles, seeded and minced
- 1 tablespoon grated fresh ginger
- 1 large russet potato, cut into ½-inch dice
- 1 medium eggplant, peeled and cut into ½-inch dice
- 8 ounces green beans, cut into 1-inch pieces
- 2 cups small cauliflower florets
- 1½cups vegetable broth
- 1 (14.5-ounce) can crushed tomatoes
- 2 tablespoons soy sauce
- ½ teaspoon ground turmeric
- 1 (13.5-ounce) can unsweetened coconut milk
- 1 tablespoon tamarind paste
- 1 tablespoon light brown sugar
- Salt and freshly ground black pepper
- 2 tablespoons fresh lime juice
- 3 tablespoons minced fresh cilantro
- 2 tablespoons minced scallions, for garnish

Directions:

1. Heat the oil in a large saucepan over medium heat. Add the onion, garlic, chilli and ginger. Cover and cook until softened for about 7 minutes.

2. Add the potato, eggplant, green beans, cauliflower, stock, tomatoes, soy sauce and turmeric. Cover and cook until vegetables are tender, stirring occasionally for about 45 minutes.

3. Finish and serve

4. Discover, lower the heat and add the coconut milk, tamarind paste, sugar, salt and pepper. The amount of salt needed depends on the salinity of the broth. Simmer uncovered until the sauce thickens, stirring occasionally for about 10 minutes. Add the lime juice. Serve hot, sprinkled with cilantro and scallions, if you have any.

Moroccan Salad

Prep Time: 30 min   **Cooking Time:** 15 min   **Servings:** 2

Ingredients:

- 1 teaspoon extra-virgin olive oil
- 1 eggplant, diced
- ½ teaspoon ground cumin
- ½ teaspoon ground ginger
- ¼ teaspoon turmeric
- ¼ teaspoon ground nutmeg
- Pinch sea salt
- 1 lemon, half zested and juiced, half cut into wedges
- 2 tablespoons capers
- 1 tablespoon chopped green olives
- 1 garlic clove, pressed
- Handful fresh mint, finely chopped
- 2 cups spinach, chopped

Directions:

1. Heat the oil in a large skillet over medium heat, then brown the aubergines. Once it has softened slightly, add the cumin, ginger, turmeric, nutmeg and salt.

2. Cook until the aubergines are very soft for about 10 minutes.

3. Add the lemon zest and juice, capers, olives, garlic and mint.

4. Sauté for another minute or two to blend the flavors.

5. Finish and serve

6. Place a handful of spinach on each plate and pour the eggplant mixture over it.

7. Serve with a lemon wedge, then squeeze the fresh juice onto the vegetables.

8. To soften the eggplant and reduce some of its natural bitter taste, you can sweat the eggplant by salting them. After cutting the aubergines into cubes, sprinkle them with salt and let them rest in a colander for about 30 minutes. Rinse the aubergines to remove the salt, then continue with the recipe as written.

Per Serving:

Calories: 97; Protein: 4g; Total fat: 4g; Carbohydrates: 16; Fiber: 8g

Moroccan Vegetable

Prep Time: 5 min   **Cooking Time:** 35 min   **Servings:** 4-6

Ingredients:

- 1 tablespoon extra-virgin olive oil
- 1 small onion, chopped
- 1 large carrot, chopped
- 1 celery rib, chopped
- 3 small zucchini, cut into ¼-inch dice
- 1 (28-ounce) can diced tomatoes, drained
- 2 tablespoons tomato paste
- 1½cups cooked or 1 (15.5-ounce) can chickpeas, drained and rinsed
- 2 teaspoons smoked paprika
- 1 teaspoon ground cumin
- 1 teaspoon za'atar spice (optional)
- ¼ teaspoon ground cayenne
- 6 cups vegetable broth, homemade or store-bought, or water
- Salt
- 4 ounces vermicelli
- 2 tablespoons minced fresh cilantro, for garnish

Directions:

1. In a large saucepan, heat the oil over medium heat. Add the onion, carrot and celery. Cover and cook until softened for about 5 minutes. Stir in the courgettes, tomatoes, tomato paste, chickpeas, paprika, cumin, za'atar and cayenne pepper. Add the broth and season with salt. Bring to a boil, then lower the heat to low and simmer, uncovered, until the vegetables are tender for about 30 minutes.

2. Finish and serve

3. Just before serving, add the vermicelli and cook until the noodles are tender for about 5 minutes. Pour the soup into bowls, garnish with cilantro, then serve.

Golden Carrot and Cauliflower Soup

Prep Time: 15 min   **Cooking Time:** 35 min   **Servings:** 4

Ingredients:

- 1 onion, chopped
- 1 tablespoon minced peeled fresh ginger or 1 teaspoon ground ginger
- 1 teaspoon extra-virgin olive oil
- 5 or 6 carrots, scrubbed or peeled and chopped
- 1 head cauliflower, chopped into florets
- ½ (13.5-ounce) can coconut milk (about ¾ cup)
- 3 cups water or unsalted vegetable broth
- ½ teaspoon ground turmeric
- ¼ to ½ teaspoon salt, plus more as needed
- Freshly ground black pepper

Directions:

1. On your electric pressure cooker, select Sauté. Add the onion, ginger and olive oil. Cook for 4-5 minutes, stirring occasionally until the onion has softened. Add the carrots, cauliflower, coconut milk, water, turmeric, and salt. Cancel Sauté.

2. High pressure for 7 minutes. Close and lock the lid. Make sure the pressure valve is sealed, then select High pressure and set the time for 7 minutes.

3. Pressure release. Once the cooking time is over, let the pressure naturally release for about 20 minutes. Once all pressure has been released, carefully unlock and remove the lid. Let it cool for a few minutes, then blend the soup - use an immersion blender directly into the pot or transfer it (in batches if necessary) to a counter-top blender. Taste and season with more salt and pepper if needed.

Per Serving:

Calories: 176; Protein: 4g; Total fat: 11g; Carbohydrates: 16; Fiber: 6g

Chickpea Soup

Prep Time: 10 min   **Cooking Tim:** 10 min   **Servings:** 7

Ingredients:

- 2 carrots, peeled and chopped
- 4 celery stalks, chopped
- 6 cups Vegetable Broth or store-bought vegetable broth
- 7 to 8 cups water
- 8 ounces spaghetti or thin brown rice noodles, broken (2 cups)
- 1 (15-ounce) can chickpeas, drained and rinsed, or 1½ cups cooked chickpeas
- 1 teaspoon dried herbs
- ¼ to ½ teaspoon salt
- Freshly ground black pepper

Directions:

1. In a large pot, combine the carrots, celery, vegetable broth and water. Bring to a boil over medium heat, then add the spaghetti, chickpeas, dried aromatic herbs, ¼ teaspoon of salt (or ½ teaspoon if the broth is not salty) and some ground pepper.

2. Cook for 8-10 minutes, until the noodles are soft.

3. Finish and serve

4. Leftovers can be stored in an airtight container in the refrigerator for up to 1 week or in the freezer for up to 1 month.

Potato and Leek Soup

Prep Time: 10 min   **Cooking Time:** 15 min   **Servings:** 4

Ingredients:

- 2 tablespoons extra-virgin olive oil
- 3 leeks, thinly sliced and thoroughly cleaned
- 2 cups cubed yukon gold potatoes (1-inch cubes)
- 5 cups vegetable stock
- 1 teaspoon sea salt
- ½ teaspoon freshly ground black pepper
- 3 tablespoons chopped fresh chives

Directions:

1. In a large saucepan over medium-high heat, heat the extra virgin olive oil until it shines.
2. Add the leeks and cook until softened for about 5 minutes.
3. Add the potatoes, vegetable stock, salt and pepper, then cook until the potatoes have softened.
4. Finish and serve
5. Transfer the soup to a blender, food processor, or hand blender and blend. Taste and adjust the toppings. Serve hot, topped with chives.

Cream of Mushroom

Prep Time: 10 min   **Cooking Time:** 20 min   **Servings:** 2

Ingredients:

- 1 to 2 teaspoons extra-virgin olive oil
- 1 onion, chopped
- 2 garlic cloves, minced
- 2 cups chopped mushrooms
- Pinch salt
- 2 tablespoons whole-wheat flour
- 1 teaspoon dried herbs
- 4 cups Vegetable Broth, store-bought broth, or water
- 1½ cups nondairy milk
- Pinch freshly ground black pepper

Directions:

1. Heat the olive oil in a large saucepan over medium-high heat.

2. Add the onion, garlic, mushrooms and salt. Sauté for about 5 minutes, until softened. Sprinkle the flour on the Shopping List: into the pot and toss to combine.

3. Cook for 1 or 2 minutes more to toast the flour.

4. Add the dried herbs, vegetable broth, milk and pepper.

5. Lower the heat and let the broth simmer. (Do not bring to a full boil or the milk may separate.)

6. Finish and serve

7. Cook for 10 minutes, until slightly thickened. Leftovers can be stored in an airtight container for up to 1 week in the refrigerator or up to 1 month in the freezer.

Per Serving:

Calories: 127; Protein: 4g; Total fat: 4g; Saturated fat: 0g; Carbohydrates: 21g; Fiber: 3g

Potato Soup

Prep Time: 5 min   **Cooking Time:** 45 min   **Servings:** 6

Ingredients:

- 2 tablespoons extra-virgin olive oil
- 1 medium red onion, chopped
- 1 medium leek, white part only, well rinsed and chopped
- 2 garlic cloves, minced
- 6 cups vegetable broth, homemade or store-bought, or water
- 1 pound red potatoes, unpeeled and cut into ½-inch dice
- 1 pound sweet potatoes, peeled and cut into ½-inch dice
- ¼ teaspoon crushed red pepper
- Salt and freshly ground black pepper
- 1 medium bunch rainbow chard, tough stems removed and coarsely chopped

Directions:

1. In a large saucepan, heat the oil over medium heat. Add the onion, leek and garlic. Cover and cook until softened for about 5 minutes. Add the broth, potatoes and chopped red pepper, then bring to a boil. Reduce the heat to low, season with salt and black pepper and simmer, uncovered, for 15 minutes.

2. Finish and serve

3. Stir in the chard and cook until the vegetables are tender for about 15 minutes, then serve.

Tofu Soup

Prep Time: 40 min   **Cooking Time:** 15 min   **Servings:** 3

Ingredients:

- 6 to 7 ounces firm or extra-firm tofu
- 1 teaspoon extra-virgin olive oil
- 1 cup sliced mushrooms
- 1 cup finely chopped cabbage
- 1 garlic clove, minced
- ½-inch piece fresh ginger, peeled and minced
- Salt
- 4 cups water or Vegetable Broth
- 2 tablespoons rice vinegar or apple cider vinegar
- 2 tablespoons soy sauce
- 1 teaspoon toasted sesame oil
- 1 teaspoon sugar
- Pinch red pepper flakes
- 1 scallion, white and light green parts only, chopped

Directions:

1. Press the tofu before you start: Place it between several layers of paper towels and place a heavy pan or book on top (with a waterproof cover or protected with cling film). Let it sit for 30 minutes. Discard the paper towels. Cut the tofu into 1/2 inch cubes.

2. In a large saucepan, heat the olive oil over medium-high heat.

3. Add the mushrooms, cabbage, garlic, ginger and a pinch of salt. Saute for 7-8 minutes until the vegetables have softened.

4. Add the water, vinegar, soy sauce, sesame oil, sugar, chilli flakes and tofu.

5. Bring to a boil, then lower the heat.

6. Finish and serve

7. Boil the soup for 5-10 minutes.

8. Serve with the shallot sprinkled on top.

9. Leftovers can be stored in an airtight container for up to 1 week in the refrigerator or up to 1 month in the freezer.

Per Serving (2 cups):

Calories: 161; Protein: 13g; Total fat: 9g; Saturated fat: 1g;

Carbohydrates: 10g; Fiber: 3g

Autumn Medley Stew

Prep Time: 5 min   **Cooking Time:** 60 min   **Servings:** 4-6

Ingredients:

- 2 tablespoons extra-virgin olive oil
- 8 ounces seitan, homemade or store-bought, cut in 1-inch cubes
- Salt and freshly ground black pepper
- 1 large yellow onion, chopped
- 2 garlic cloves, minced
- 1 large russet potato, peeled and cut into ½-inch dice
- 1 medium carrot, cut into ¼-inch dice
- 1 medium parsnip, cut into ¼-inch dice chopped
- 1 small butternut squash, peeled, halved, seeded, and cut into ½-inch dice
- 1 small head savoy cabbage, chopped
- 1 (14.5-ounce) can diced tomatoes, drained
- 1½cups cooked or 1 (15.5-ounce) can chickpeas, drained and rinsed
- 2 cups vegetable broth,
- ½ cup dry white wine
- ½ teaspoon dried marjoram
- ½ teaspoon dried thyme
- ½ cup crumbled angel hair pasta

Directions:

1. In a large skillet, heat 1 tablespoon of oil over medium-high heat. Add the seitan and cook until golden brown on all sides for about 5 minutes. Season with salt and pepper and set aside.

2. In a large saucepan, heat the remaining 1 tablespoon of oil over medium heat. Add the onion and garlic. Cover and cook until softened for 5 minutes. Add the potato, carrot, parsnip and pumpkin. Cover and cook until softened for about 10 minutes.

3. Mix the cabbage, tomatoes, chickpeas, broth, wine, marjoram, thyme, salt and pepper. Bring to a boil, then reduce the heat to low. Cover and cook, stirring occasionally until the vegetables are tender for about 45 minutes.

4. Finish and serve

5. Add the cooked seitan and pasta, then simmer until the pasta is tender and the flavors have blended for about 10 more minutes. Serve immediately

Pumpkin- Pear Soup

Prep Time: 10 min **Cooking Time:** 15 min **Servings:** 4

Ingredients:

- 1 teaspoon extra-virgin olive oil or coconut oil
- 1 onion, diced, or 2 teaspoons onion powder
- 1-inch piece fresh ginger, peeled and diced, or 1 teaspoon ground ginger
- 1 pear, cored and chopped
- Optional spices to take the taste up a notch:
- 1 teaspoon curry powder
- ½ teaspoon pumpkin pie spice
- ½ teaspoon smoked paprika
- Pinch red pepper flakes
- 4 cups water or Vegetable Broth
- 3 cups canned pumpkin purée
- 1 to 2 teaspoons salt (less if using salted broth)
- Pinch freshly ground black pepper
- ¼ to ½ cup canned coconut milk (optional)
- 2 to 4 tablespoons nutritional yeast (optional)

Directions:

1. Heat the olive oil in a large saucepan over medium heat. Add the onion, ginger and pear, then sauté for about 5 minutes until softened. Sprinkle with optional spices and toss to combine.

2. Add the water, squash, salt and pepper, then mix until smooth and combine. Cook until boiling for about 10 minutes.

3. Finish and serve

4. Stir in the coconut milk (if used) and nutritional yeast (if used) and remove the soup from the heat. Leftovers can be stored in an airtight container for up to 1 week in the refrigerator or up to 1 month in the freezer.

Sweet Potato & Peanut Soup

Prep Time: 5 min   **Cooking Time:** 40 min   **Servings:** 4

Ingredients:

- 1 tablespoon extra-virgin olive oil
- 1 medium onion, chopped
- 1½ pounds sweet potatoes, peeled and cut into ½-inch dice
- 6 cups vegetable broth, or water
- 1/3 cup creamy peanut butter
- ¼ teaspoon ground cayenne
- ⅛ teaspoon ground nutmeg
- Salt and freshly ground black pepper
- 4 cups fresh baby spinach

Directions:

1. In a large saucepan, heat the oil over medium heat. Add the onion, then cover and cook until softened for about 5 minutes. Add the sweet potatoes and stock and cook uncovered until the potatoes are tender for about 30 minutes.

2. Pour about a cup of hot broth into a small bowl. Add the peanut butter and mix until smooth.

3. Finish and serve

4. Mix the peanut butter mixture into the soup along with the cayenne pepper, nutmeg, salt and pepper.

5. About 10 minutes before ready to serve, stir in the spinach, then serve.

Tuscan Bean Soup

Prep Time: 10 min   **Cooking Time:** 15 min   **Servings:** 4

Ingredients:

- 1 to 2 teaspoons extra-virgin olive oil
- 1 onion, chopped
- 4 garlic cloves, minced, or 1 teaspoon garlic powder
- 2 carrots, peeled and chopped
- Salt
- 1 tablespoon dried herbs
- Pinch freshly ground black pepper
- Pinch red pepper flakes
- 4 cups Vegetable Broth or water
- 2 (15-ounce) cans white beans, such as cannellini, navy, or great northern, drained and rinsed
- 2 tablespoons freshly squeezed lemon juice
- 2 cups chopped greens, such as spinach, kale, arugula, or chard

Directions:

1. Heat the extra virgin olive oil in a large saucepan over medium-high heat.

2. Add the onion, garlic (if using fresh), carrots and a pinch of salt.

3. Sauté for about 5 minutes, stirring occasionally until the vegetables are lightly browned. Sprinkle the dried herbs (plus powdered garlic if using), black pepper, and red pepper flakes, then stir to combine.

4. Add the vegetable stock, beans and another pinch of salt, then bring the soup to a boil. If desired, make the broth a little creamier by blending 1 to 2 cups of the soup in a counter-top blender and returning it to the pot. Alternatively, use a hand blender to puree about a quarter of the beans in the pot.

5. Finish and serve

6. Mix the lemon juice and vegetables and let the vegetables wilt in the soup before serving. Leftovers can be stored in an airtight container for up to 1 week in the refrigerator or up to 1 month in the freezer.

Per Serving (2 cups) :

Calories: 145; Protein: 7g; Total fat: 2g; Saturated fat: 0g; Carbohydrates: 26g; Fiber: 6g

Mexican Fideo Soup

Prep Time: 5 min   **Cooking Time:** 25 min   **Servings:** 4

Ingredients:

- 3 tablespoons extra-virgin olive oil
- 1 medium onion, chopped
- 3 garlic cloves, chopped
- 8 ounces fideo, vermicelli, or angel hair pasta, broken into 2-inch pieces
- 1 (14.5-ounce) can crushed tomatoes
- 1½ cups cooked or 1 (15.5-ounce) can pinto beans, rinsed and drained
- 1 (4-ounce) can chopped hot or mild green chiles
- 1 teaspoon ground cumin
- ½ teaspoon dried oregano
- 6 cups vegetable broth, homemade (see Light Vegetable Broth) or store-bought, or water
- Salt and freshly ground black pepper
- ¼ cup chopped fresh cilantro, for garnish

Directions:

1. In a large saucepan, heat 1 tablespoon of oil over medium heat. Add the onion, cover and cook until soft for about 10 minutes. Incorporate the garlic and cook 1 minute more. Remove the onion mixture with a slotted spoon and set aside.

2. In the same pot, heat the remaining 2 tablespoons of oil over medium heat, add the noodles and cook until golden brown, stirring often for 5-7 minutes. Be careful not to burn the noodles.

3. Finish and serve.

4. Stir in the tomatoes, beans, chillies, cumin, oregano, broth, salt and pepper. Stir in the onion mixture and simmer until the vegetables and noodles are tender, for 10-15 minutes. Pour into soup bowls, garnish with cilantro, then serve.

Spinach, Tomato, and Orzo Soup

Prep Time: 10 min   **Cooking Time:** 20 min   **Servings:** 6

Ingredients:

- 1 tablespoon extra-virgin olive oil
- 1 onion, chopped
- 4 garlic cloves, minced
- 1 (14.5-ounce) can diced Italian tomatoes (preferably with oregano and basil)
- 4 cups low-sodium vegetable broth
- 4 cups water
- 1 teaspoon sea salt
- 1 teaspoon black pepper
- 1 pound uncooked orzo pasta
- 1 (5-ounce) package baby spinach

Directions:

1.
2. Heat the oil in a large saucepan over medium heat. Add the onion and sauté for 3 minutes or until soft. Add the garlic and sauté for 1 more minute or until fragrant. Add the tomatoes with their juice, broth, water, salt and pepper. Cover the pot and bring to a boil. Reduce the heat to a boil.
3. Add the barley and cook, uncovered, for 9 minutes or until the pasta is tender.
4. Finish and serve
5. Turn off the heat and stir in the spinach until they wilt.

Black Bean Soup

Prep Time: 5 min   **Cooking Time:** 45 min   **Servings:** 4-6

Ingredients:

- 1 tablespoon extra-virgin olive oil
- 1 medium onion, finely chopped
- 1 celery rib, finely chopped
- 2 medium carrots, finely chopped
- 1 small green bell pepper, finely chopped
- 2 garlic cloves, minced
- 4 cups vegetable broth, or water
- 4½ cups cooked or 3 (15.5-ounce) cans black beans, drained and rinsed
- 1 teaspoon dried thyme
- 1 teaspoon salt
- ¼ teaspoon ground cayenne
- 2 tablespoons minced fresh parsley, for garnish
- 1/3 cup dry sherry

Directions:

1. In a large saucepan, heat the oil over medium heat. Add the onion, celery, carrots, pepper and garlic. Cover and cook until tender, stirring occasionally for about 10 minutes. Add the stock, beans, thyme, salt and cayenne pepper. Bring to a boil, then reduce the heat to low and simmer, uncovered, until the soup has thickened for about 45 minutes.

2. Finish and serve

3. Blend the soup in the pot with an immersion blender or in a blender or food processor, in batches if necessary, and return it to the pot. Reheat if necessary.

4. Pour the soup into bowls and garnish with parsley. Serve accompanied by sherry.

Creamy Spinach-Stuffed Mushrooms

Prep Time: 10 min   **Cooking Time:** 25 min   **Servings:** 4

Ingredients:

- 1 tablespoon extra-virgin olive oil
- 1 onion, chopped
- 3 garlic cloves, minced
- 1 (14-ounce) block extra-firm tofu, drained and crumbled
- 1 (5-ounce) package baby spinach
- 2 teaspoons Italian seasoning
- 1 teaspoon onion powder
- ½ teaspoon garlic powder
- 1 teaspoon sea salt
- ½ teaspoon black pepper
- 4 large portobello mushroom caps, stemmed

Directions:

1. Preheat the oven to 450 ° F. Line a baking sheet with parchment paper. In a large skillet, heat the oil over medium heat.

2. Add the onion and sauté for 3 minutes or until soft.

3. Add the garlic and sauté for 1 more minute or until fragrant. Stir in the crumbled tofu and spinach, then cook for 3 minutes or until the spinach is wilted.

4. Add the Italian seasoning, onion powder, garlic powder, salt and pepper. Mix until well combined. Place the mushroom caps on the prepared baking sheet, top side down. Divide the tofu mixture between the 4 mushroom caps.

5. Bake

6. Cook for 15-20 minutes until the filling is lightly golden.

Squash Soup

Prep Time: 10 min   **Cooking Time:** 20 min   **Servings:** 5

Ingredients:

- 1 butternut squash (roughly 2 pounds), peeled, seeded, and cut into ½-inch cubes
- 1 red bell pepper, seeded and chopped
- 1 large onion, chopped
- 3 garlic cloves, minced
- 4 cups low-sodium vegetable broth
- Juice of ½ lemon
- 2 tablespoons maple syrup
- ¾ teaspoon salt
- ¾ teaspoon black pepper

Directions:

1. In a large pot, combine the pumpkin, pepper, onion, garlic and broth.
2. Stir well to mix, cover and bring to a boil.
3. Reduce to low heat and cook, covered, for 15 minutes or until squash is tender. Add the lemon juice, maple syrup, salt and pepper and mix well to combine.
4. Finish and serve
5. Carefully transfer the soup to a blender. Remove the plug from the blender lid to allow the steam to escape, hold a towel firmly on the lid hole and blend until smooth.
6. Start at the slowest speed possible and gradually increase until the soup is completely smooth. Depending on the capacity of the blender, this may need to be done in two batches. (If you have an immersion blender, it would work great here.) Gently reheat over low heat to serve.

Cream of Tomato Soup

Prep Time: 5 min   **Cooking Time:** 5 min   **Servings:** 2

Ingredients:

- 1 (28-ounce) can crushed, diced, or whole peeled tomatoes, undrained
- 1 to 2 teaspoons dried herbs
- 2 to 3 teaspoons onion powder (optional)
- ¾ to 1 cup unsweetened nondairy milk
- ½ teaspoon salt, or to taste
- Freshly ground black pepper

Directions:

1. Pour the tomatoes and their juice into a large pot and bring them almost to a boil over medium heat.

2. Add the dried herbs, onion powder (if used), milk, salt and pepper to taste. Stir to combine.

3. Finish and serve

4. If you used whole or diced tomatoes, use a hand blender to blend the soup until smooth. (Alternatively, let the soup cool for a few minutes, then transfer to an over-the-counter blender.) Leftovers store in an airtight container for up to 1 week in the refrigerator or up to 1 month in the freezer.

Per Serving (2 cups) :

Calories: 90; Protein: 4g; Total fat: 3g; Saturated fat: 0g; Carbohydrates: 16g; Fiber: 4g

Succotash Stew

Prep Time: 5 min   **Cooking Time:** 60 min   **Servings:** 4

Ingredients:

- 8 ounces tempeh
- 2 tablespoons extra-virgin olive oil
- 1 large sweet yellow onion, finely chopped
- 2 medium russet potatoes, peeled and cut into ½-inch dice
- 2 carrots, cut into ¼-inch slices
- 1 (14.5-ounce) can diced tomatoes, drained
- 1 (16-ounce) package frozen succotash
- 2 cups vegetable broth or water
- 2 tablespoons soy sauce
- 1 teaspoon dry mustard
- ½ teaspoon dried thyme
- ½ teaspoon ground allspice
- ¼ teaspoon ground cayenne
- Salt and freshly ground black pepper
- ½ teaspoon liquid smoke

Directions:

1. In a medium saucepan of boiling water, cook the tempeh for 30 minutes. Drain, pat dry and cut into 1-inch cubes.

2. In a large skillet, heat 1 tablespoon of oil over medium heat. Add the tempeh and cook until golden on both sides for about 10 minutes. To put aside.

3. In a large saucepan, heat the remaining 1 tablespoon of oil over medium heat. Add the onion and cook until softened for 5 minutes. Add the potatoes, carrots, tomatoes, succotash, broth, soy sauce, mustard, sugar, thyme, allspice, and cayenne pepper. Season with salt and pepper. Bring to a boil, then lower the heat and add the tempeh. Simmer, covered, until vegetables are tender, stirring occasionally for about 45 minutes.

4. Finish and serve

5. About 10 minutes before the stew is done, stir in the liquid smoke. Taste and adjust toppings as needed. Serve immediately.

Thai Mushroom Soup

Prep Time: 5 min   **Cooking Time:** 10 min   **Servings:** 4

Ingredients:

- 1½ cups low-sodium vegetable broth, divided
- 2 garlic cloves, minced
- 1 tablespoon minced fresh ginger
- 1 (8-ounce) package baby bella or white button mushrooms, stemmed and sliced
- 1 (13.5-ounce) can full-fat coconut milk
- Juice of ½ lemon
- Juice of ½ lime
- 2 tablespoons chopped fresh Thai basil
- 1 tablespoon chopped fresh cilantro
- Fresh cilantro leaves, for garnish (optional)
- Lime wedges, for garnish (optional)

Directions:

1. Heat 1/2 cup of broth in a large saucepan over medium-high heat. Saute the garlic and ginger in the broth for 1 minute or until they are fragrant.

2. Add the mushrooms and slowly pour in the remaining cup of broth. Bring to a boil and reduce the heat to a boil. Add the coconut milk, lemon juice, lime juice, basil and chopped cilantro.

3. Finish and serve

4. Let it simmer for 5 minutes or until it warms up. Garnish with whole coriander leaves and lime wedges if desired.

Spicy Black Bean Soup

Prep Time: 5 min   **Cooking Time:** 50 min   **Servings:** 4-6

Ingredients:

- 2 tablespoons extra-virgin olive oil
- 3 garlic cloves, minced
- 1 tablespoon chili powder
- 1 teaspoon dried oregano
- 4½ cups cooked or 3 (15.5-ounce) cans black beans, drained and rinsed
- 1 small jalapeño, seeded and finely chopped (optional)
- ¼ cup minced oil-packed sun-dried tomatoes
- 4 cups vegetable broth, or water
- 1 cup water
- Salt and freshly ground black pepper
- ½ cup orzo
- 2 tablespoons chopped fresh cilantro, for garnish

Directions:

1. In a large saucepan, heat the oil over medium heat. Add the garlic and cook until fragrant for about 1 minute. Stir in the chili powder, oregano, beans (jalapeño if using), tomatoes, stock, water, salt, and pepper. Simmer for 30 minutes to blend the flavors.

2. Place the soup in the pot with an immersion blender, or in a blender or food processor - in batches if necessary - then return to the pot. Cook the soup for 15 more minutes over medium heat. Taste and adjust toppings, adding more water as needed.

3. Finish and serve

4. While the soup is simmering, cook the barley in a pot of boiling salted water, stirring occasionally until al dente for about 5 minutes. Drain the barley and divide it into bowls. Pour the soup into bowls, garnish with cilantro, then serve.

Root Vegetable Soup

Prep Time: 15 min   **Cooking Time:** 15 min   **Servings:** 4

Ingredients:

- 2 tablespoons extra-virgin olive oil
- 1 onion, diced
- 3 garlic cloves, minced
- 1 carrot, julienned or grated
- 1 rutabaga, julienned or grated
- 1 parsnip, julienned or grated
- 1 red potato, julienned or grated
- 5 cups vegetable stock
- 2 teaspoons dried thyme
- sea salt
- freshly ground black pepper

Directions:

1. In a large saucepan, heat the olive oil over medium-high heat until it glows.

2. Add the onion and cook until softened for about 5 minutes. Add the garlic and cook until fragrant. Add the carrot, rutabaga, parsnip, potato, vegetable stock and thyme. Cover and boil until the vegetables soften for about 10 minutes.

3. Finish and serve

4. Remove from the heat. Using a food processor or blender, blend the soup in batches. Season with salt and pepper. Serve immediately.

Minestrone

Prep Time: 15 min **Cooking Time:** 15 min **Servings:** 4

Ingredients:

- 2 tablespoons extra-virgin olive oil
- ½ onion, diced
- 1 carrot, peeled and diced
- 1 stalk celery, diced
- 4 garlic cloves, minced
- 5 cups vegetable stock
- 1 zucchini, diced
- one 15-ounce can kidney beans, drained and rinsed
- one 15-ounce can chopped tomatoes with liquid, or 2 fresh tomatoes, peeled and chopped
- 2 teaspoons italian seasoning
- sea salt
- freshly ground pepper

Directions:

1. In a large saucepan, heat the olive oil over medium-high heat until it glows.

2. Add the onion, carrot and celery and cook until the vegetables soften for about 5 minutes. Add the garlic and cook until fragrant. Add the vegetable stock, courgettes, beans, tomatoes and the Italian dressing. Simmer the soup until the vegetables are soft for about 10 minutes.

3. Finish and serve

4. Season with salt and pepper, then serve immediately.

Veggie Stew

Prep Time: 5 min   **Cooking Time:** 55 min   **Servings:** 4

Ingredients:

- 1 tablespoon extra-virgin olive oil
- 1 large onion, chopped
- 1 medium eggplant, peeled and cut into ½-inch dice
- 2 medium carrots, cut into ¼-inch slices
- 1 large Yukon Gold potato, peeled and cut into ½-inch dice
- 1 medium red bell pepper, cut into 1-inch dice
- 3 garlic cloves, minced
- 2 cups cooked or 1 (15.5-ounce) cans chickpeas, drained and rinsed if canned
- 1 (28-ounce) can diced tomatoes, undrained
- 1 tablespoon minced fresh parsley
- ½ teaspoon dried oregano
- ½ teaspoon dried basil
- 1 tablespoon soy sauce
- ½ cup vegetable broth, or water
- Salt and freshly ground black pepper

Directions:

1. In a large saucepan, heat the oil over medium heat. Add the onion, eggplant and carrots, cover and cook until the vegetables begin to soften for about 5 minutes.

2. Reduce the heat to a minimum. Add the potato, pepper and garlic and cook, stirring, uncovered, for about 5 minutes. Incorporate the chickpeas, tomatoes, parsley, oregano, basil, soy sauce and stock.

3. Finish and serve

4. Season with salt and black pepper. Cover and cook until vegetables are tender for about 45 minutes. Serve immediately.

Tomato Cream Pasta

Prep Time: 10 min   **Cooking Time:** 15 min   **Servings:** 4

Ingredients:

- 1 (28-ounce) can crushed tomatoes
- 1 tablespoon dried basil
- ½ teaspoon garlic powder
- 10 ounces whole-grain pasta
- ½ teaspoon salt, plus more as needed
- 1½ cups water or unsalted vegetable broth
- 1 cup unsweetened nondairy milk or creamer
- 2 cups chopped fresh spinach (optional)
- Freshly ground black pepper

Directions:

1. In your electric pressure cooking pot, combine the tomatoes, basil, garlic powder, pasta, salt, and water.

2. High pressure for 4 minutes Lock the lid and ensure the pressure valve is sealed, then select High Pressure and set the time for 4 minutes.

3. Pressure Release Once the cook time is complete, let the pressure release naturally for 5 minutes, then quickly release any remaining pressure. Once all the pressure has been released, carefully unlock and remove the lid.

4. Stir in the milk and spinach (if using). Taste and season with more salt if needed, and pepper. On your pressure cooker, select Sauté or Simmer. Let it cook for 4 to 5 minutes until the sauce thickens and the greens wilt.

Per Serving:

Calories: 321; Protein: 14g; Total fat: 3g; Saturated fat: 0g; Carbohydrates: 16g; Fiber: 9g

Three Bean Soup

Prep Time: 5 min   **Cooking Time:** 52 min   **Servings:** 4-6

Ingredients:

- 2 tablespoons extra-virgin olive oil
- 1 medium onion, chopped
- 1 medium carrot, chopped
- 1 cup chopped celery
- 2 garlic cloves, minced
- 1 (14.5-ounce) can diced tomatoes, drained
- 1½ cups cooked or 1 (15.5-ounce) can dark red kidney beans, drained and rinsed
- 1½ cups cooked or 1 (15.5-ounce) can black beans, drained and rinsed
- 1½ cups cooked or 1 (15.5-ounce) can navy or other white beans, drained and rinsed
- 4 cups vegetable broth, homemade (see Light Vegetable Broth) or store-bought, or water
- 1 tablespoon soy sauce
- 1 teaspoon dried thyme
- 1 bay leaf
- Salt and freshly ground black pepper
- 2 tablespoons chopped fresh parsley

Directions:

1. In a large saucepan, heat the oil over medium heat. Add the onion, carrot, celery and garlic. Cover and cook until softened for about 7 minutes. Uncover and mix in the tomatoes, all the beans and the broth. Add the soy sauce, thyme and bay leaf, then season with salt and pepper. Bring to a boil, then reduce the heat to low and simmer until the vegetables are tender for about 45 minutes.

2. Finish and serve

3. Remove the bay leaf and discard before serving. Add the parsley and serve.

Potato-Cauliflower Soup

Prep Time: 10 min   **Cooking Time:** 25 min   **Servings:** 6

Ingredients:

- 1 teaspoon extra-virgin olive oil
- 1 onion, chopped
- 3 cups chopped cauliflower
- 2 potatoes, scrubbed or peeled and chopped
- 6 cups water or Vegetable Broth
- 2 tablespoons dried herbs
- Salt
- Freshly ground black pepper
- 1 or 2 scallions, white and light green parts only, sliced

Directions:

1. Heat the olive oil in a large saucepan over medium-high heat.

2. Add the onion and cauliflower and sauté for about 5 minutes, until the vegetables are slightly softened. Add the potatoes, water and dried herbs and season to taste with salt and pepper. Bring the soup to a boil, lower the heat and cover the pot. Simmer for 15-20 minutes, until the potatoes are soft.

3. Finish and serve

4. Using a hand blender, blend the soup until smooth. (Alternatively, allow to cool slightly, then transfer to an over-the-counter blender.) Stir in the shallots and serve. Leftovers can be stored in an airtight container for up to 1 week in the refrigerator or up to 1 month in the freezer.

Per Serving (2 cups) :

Calories: 80; Protein: 2g; Total fat: 1g; Saturated fat: 0g; Carbohydrates: 17g; Fiber: 3g

Coconut and Curry Soup

Prep Time: 15 min   **Cooking Time:** 15 min   **Servings:** 4

Ingredients:

- 1 tablespoon coconut oil
- ½ onion, thinly sliced
- 1 carrot, peeled and julienned
- ½ cup sliced shiitake mushrooms
- 3 garlic cloves, minced
- one 14-ounce can coconut milk
- 1 cup vegetable stock
- juice from 1 lime, or 2 teaspoons lime juice
- ½ teaspoon sea salt
- 2 teaspoons curry powder

Directions:

1. In a large saucepan, heat the coconut oil over medium-high heat until it glows. Add the onion, carrot and mushrooms, then cook until soft for about 7 minutes. Incorporate the garlic and cook until fragrant.

2. Finish and serve

3. Add the coconut milk, vegetable stock, lime juice, salt and curry powder, then heat. Serve immediately.

Gazpacho

Prep Time: 15 min **Cooking Time:** 0 min **Servings:** 4

Ingredients:

- 1½ pounds ripe yellow tomatoes, chopped
- 1 large cucumber, peeled, seeded, and chopped
- 1 large yellow bell pepper, seeded, and chopped
- 4 green onions, white part only
- 2 garlic cloves, minced
- 2 tablespoons extra-virgin olive oil
- 2 tablespoons white wine vinegar
- Salt
- Ground cayenne
- 1½ cups cooked or 1 (15.5-ounce) can black beans, drained and rinsed
- 2 tablespoons minced fresh parsley
- 1 cup toasted croutons (optional)

Directions:

1. In a blender or food processor, combine half of the tomatoes with the cucumber, bell pepper, green onions, and garlic. Blend until smooth. Add the oil and vinegar, season with salt and cayenne pepper, then blend until smooth.

2. Finish and serve

3. Transfer the soup to a large non-metallic bowl and stir in the remaining black beans and tomatoes. Cover the bowl and refrigerate for 1 to 2 hours. Taste and adjust toppings as needed.

4. Pour the soup into bowls, garnish with parsley and croutons if used, then serve.

Sweet Potato Soup

Prep Time: 10 min   **Cooking Time:** 25 min   **Servings:** 4

Ingredients:

- 1 teaspoon extra-virgin olive oil
- 2 to 3 cups peeled, cubed sweet potato, squash, or pumpkin
- ½ onion, chopped
- 1 garlic clove, minced
- Salt
- 2 cups water
- 1 (15-ounce) can black-eyed peas, drained and rinsed
- 2 tablespoons freshly squeezed lime juice
- 1 tablespoon sugar
- 1 teaspoon smoked or regular paprika
- Pinch red pepper flakes or cayenne pepper
- 3 cups shredded cabbage
- 1 cup corn kernels, thawed if frozen, drained if canned

Directions:

1. Heat the olive oil in a large saucepan over medium-high heat.
2. Add the sweet potato, onion, garlic and a pinch of salt. Saute for 3-4 minutes until the onion and garlic have softened. Add the water, black-eyed peas, lime juice, sugar, paprika, chilli flakes and salt. Bring to a boil and cook for 15 minutes. Add the kale and corn to the pot, stir to combine, then cook for another 5 minutes or until the sweet potato is tender.
3. Finish and serve
4. Turn off the heat, let it cool for a few minutes and serve. Leftovers can be stored in an airtight container for up to 1 week in the refrigerator or up to 1 month in the freezer.

Per Serving (2 cups):

Calories: 224; Protein: 9g; Total fat: 2g; Saturated fat: 0g; Carbohydrates: 46g; Fiber: 10g

Lentil Soup

Prep Time: 5 min   **Cooking Time:** 55 min   **Servings:** 4-6

Ingredients:

- 2 tablespoons extra-virgin olive oil
- 1 medium onion, minced
- 1 medium carrot, halved lengthwise and sliced diagonally
- 2 garlic cloves, minced
- 1 (28-ounce) can crushed tomatoes
- 1 cup green (French) lentils, picked over, rinsed, and drained
- 1 teaspoon dried thyme
- 6 cups vegetable broth, homemade or store-bought, or water
- Salt and freshly ground black pepper
- 4 ounces soba noodles, broken into thirds

Directions:

1. In a large saucepan over medium heat, heat the oil. Add the onion, carrot and garlic. Cover and cook until softened for about 7 minutes. Uncover and mix in the tomatoes, lentils, thyme and broth, then bring to a boil. Reduce the heat to medium, season with salt and pepper, then cover and simmer until the lentils are tender. Cook for about 45 minutes.

2. Finish and serve

3. Incorporate the noodles and cook until tender for about 10 more minutes, then serve.

Senegalese Soup

Prep Time: 5 min   **Cooking Time:** 40 min   **Servings:** 4

Ingredients:

- 1 tablespoon canola or grapeseed oil
- 1 medium onion, chopped
- 1 medium carrot, chopped
- 1 garlic clove, minced
- 3 Granny Smith apples, peeled, cored, and chopped
- 2 tablespoons hot or mild curry powder
- 2 teaspoons tomato paste
- 3 cups light vegetable broth, homemade (see Light Vegetable Broth) or store-bought, or water
- Salt
- 1 cup plain unsweetened soy milk
- 4 teaspoons mango chutney, homemade or store-bought, for garnish

Directions:

1. In a large saucepan, heat the oil over medium heat. Add the onion, carrot and garlic. Cover and cook until softened for about 10 minutes. Add the apples and continue cooking, uncovered, stirring occasionally until the apples begin to soften for about 5 minutes. Add the curry powder and cook, stirring for 1 minute. Incorporate the tomato paste, broth and salt. Simmer, uncovered, for 30 minutes.

2. Finish and serve

3. Pu r é e soup into the pot with an immersion blender or food processor, in batches as needed. Pour the soup into a large container, stir in the soy milk, cover and refrigerate until it cools for about 3 hours.

4. Pour the soup into the bowls. Garnish each with a teaspoon of chutney, then serve.

Chickpea Stew

Prep Time: 5 min   **Cooking Time:** 60 min   **Servings:** 4

Ingredients:

- 1 tablespoon extra-virgin olive oil
- 1 large onion, chopped
- 2 medium Yukon Gold potatoes, peeled and cut into 1/4-inch dice
- 3 cups cooked chickpeas or 2 (15.5-ounce) cans chickpeas, drained and rinsed
- 1 (28-ounce) can crushed tomatoes
- 1 (4-ounce) can mild chopped green chiles, drained
- 2 tablespoons tamarind paste
- 1/4 cup pure maple syrup
- 1 cup vegetable broth, homemade or water
- 2 tablespoons chili powder
- 1 teaspoon ground coriander
- 1/2 teaspoon ground cumin
- Salt and freshly ground black pepper
- 1 cup frozen baby peas, thawed

Directions:

1. In a large saucepan, heat the oil over medium heat. Add the onion, cover and cook until softened for about 5 minutes. Add the potatoes, chickpeas, tomatoes and chillies, then simmer, uncovered for about 5 minutes.

2. In a small bowl, combine the tamarind paste, maple syrup and broth and blend until smooth. Incorporate the tamarind mixture into the vegetables, along with the chili powder, coriander, cumin, salt, and pepper. Bring to a boil, then reduce the heat to medium and simmer, covered, until the potatoes are tender for about 40 minutes.

3. Finish and serve

4. Taste, adjusting the seasonings if necessary, and stir in the peas. Simmer, uncovered, for another 10 minutes. Serve immediately.

Black Bean Soup

Prep Time: 10 min   **Cooking Time:** 15 min   **Servings:** 4

Ingredients:

- 2 tablespoons extra-virgin olive oil
- 1 onion, diced
- 1 green bell pepper, diced
- 1 carrot, peeled and diced
- 4 garlic cloves, minced
- two 15-ounce cans black beans, drained and rinsed
- 2 cups vegetable stock
- ¼ teaspoon ground cumin
- 1 teaspoon sea salt
- ¼ cup chopped cilantro, for garnish

Directions:

1. In a large saucepan, heat the olive oil over medium-high heat until it glows.

2. Add the onion, pepper and carrot and cook until the vegetables soften for about 5 minutes. Add the garlic and cook until fragrant. Add the black beans, vegetable stock, cumin and salt. Cook over medium-high heat, stirring occasionally for about 10 minutes.

3. Finish and serve

4. Remove from the heat. Using a potato masher, lightly mash the beans and leave a few pieces in the soup. For a smoother soup, work in a blender or food processor. Serve hot, garnished with cilantro.

Spicy Bean Soup

Prep Time: 5 min **Cooking Time:** 25 min **Servings:** 4

Ingredients:

- 4½ cups cooked or 3 (15.5-ounce) cans pinto beans, drained and rinsed
- 1 (14.5-ounce) can crushed tomatoes
- 1 teaspoon chipotle chile in adobo
- 2 tablespoons extra-virgin olive oil
- 1 medium onion, chopped
- ¼ cup chopped celery
- 2 garlic cloves, minced
- ½ teaspoon ground cumin
- ½ teaspoon dried oregano
- 4 cups vegetable broth, homemade or water
- Salt and freshly ground black pepper
- 2 tablespoons chopped fresh cilantro, for garnish

Directions:

1. In a food processor, pour 1 ½ cup of pinto beans with tomatoes and chipotle. To put aside.

2. In a large saucepan, heat the oil over medium heat. Add the onion, celery and garlic. Cover and cook until soft, stirring occasionally for about 10 minutes. Stir in the cumin, oregano, stock, red bean mixture and the remaining 3 cups of beans. Season with salt and pepper.

3. Bring to a boil and lower the heat and simmer, uncovered, stirring occasionally until the flavors have incorporated and the soup is hot, about 15 minutes.

4. Finish and serve

5. Pour into bowls, garnish with cilantro, then serve.

Spinach Soup

Prep Time: 10 min   **Cooking Time:** 15 min   **Servings:** 4

Ingredients:

- 1 teaspoon extra-virgin olive oil
- 1 cup chopped mushrooms
- ¼ teaspoon plus a pinch salt
- 4 garlic cloves, minced, or 1 teaspoon garlic powder
- 2 peeled carrots or ½ red bell pepper, chopped
- 6 cups Vegetable Broth or water
- Pinch freshly ground black pepper
- 1 cup rotini or gnocchi
- ¾ cup unsweetened nondairy milk
- ¼ cup nutritional yeast
- 2 cups chopped fresh spinach
- ¼ cup pitted black olives or sun-dried tomatoes, chopped
- Herbed Croutons, for topping (optional)

Directions:

1. Heat the olive oil in a large saucepan over medium-high heat.

2. Add the mushrooms and a pinch of salt. Saute for about 4 minutes until the mushrooms soften. Add the garlic (if using fresh) and carrots, then sauté for 1 minute. Add the vegetable stock, then add the remaining ¼ teaspoon of salt and pepper (plus the garlic powder if using). Bring to a boil and add the pasta. Cook for about 10 minutes until the pasta is cooked.

3. Finish and serve

4. Turn off the heat and mix in the milk, nutritional yeast, spinach and olives. Garnish with croutons (if used). Leftovers can be stored in an airtight container for up to 1 week in the refrigerator or up to 1 month in the freezer.

Per Serving (2 cups):

Calories: 207; Protein: 11g; Total fat: 5g; Saturated fat: 1g; Carbohydrates: 34g; Fiber: 7g

Spicy Gazpacho

Prep Time: 15 min   **Cooking Time:** 0 min   **Servings:** 4

Ingredients:

- 1 tablespoon extra-virgin olive oil
- 3 cups vegetable juice
- 1 red onion, diced
- 3 tomatoes, chopped
- 1 red bell pepper, diced
- 2 garlic cloves, minced
- juice of 1 lemon
- 2 tablespoons chopped fresh basil
- ¼ to ½ teaspoon cayenne pepper
- sea salt
- freshly ground black pepper

Directions:

1. In a blender or food processor, combine the olive oil, vegetable juice, all but ½ cup of onion, all but ½ cup of tomato, all but ½ cup of bell pepper, garlic, lemon juice, basil and cayenne pepper. Season with salt and pepper, then blend until smooth.

2. Finish and serve

3. Mix ½ cup of onion, ½ cup of tomatoes and ½ cup of bell pepper into the processed grocery list: and refrigerate for 1 hour. Serve cold.

Cabbage, Carrot, and Potato Stew

Prep Time: 10 min   **Cooking Time:** 20 min   **Servings:** 6

Ingredients:

- 3 russet potatoes, peeled and cut into ½-inch cubes
- 2 tablespoons extra-virgin olive oil
- 6 carrots, peeled, halved lengthwise, and cut into ½-inch slices
- 1 onion, chopped
- 4 garlic cloves, minced
- 1 tablespoon ground turmeric
- 1 teaspoon ground cumin
- 1 teaspoon ground ginger
- 1½ teaspoons sea salt
- 1½ cups low-sodium vegetable broth, divided
- 4 cups shredded or thinly sliced green cabbage

Directions:

1. Bring a large pot of water to a boil over medium-high heat.

2. Add the potatoes and cook for 10 minutes or until tender. Drain and set aside. While the potatoes are cooking, heat the oil in a large skillet over medium-high heat. Add the carrots and onion, then sauté for 5 minutes. Add the garlic, turmeric, cumin, ginger and salt, then sauté for 1 more minute until fragrant. Add the cooked potatoes and 1 cup of broth to the pan, bring to a boil and reduce to a simmer. Sprinkle the cabbage on top of the potatoes. Cover and simmer for 3 minutes.

3. Mix the cabbage with the potatoes, add the remaining ½ cup of broth, cover and simmer for another 5 minutes, or until the cabbage is wilted and tender.

4. Finish and serve

5. Stir the cabbage from time to time during cooking to incorporate it into the other shopping list: as it continues to wilt.

Root Vegetable Bisque

Prep Time: 5 min   **Cooking Time:** 35 min   **Servings:** 4-6

Ingredients:

- 1 tablespoon extra-virgin olive oil
- 3 large shallots, chopped
- 2 large carrots, shredded
- 2 medium parsnips, shredded
- 1 medium potato, peeled and chopped
- 2 garlic cloves, minced
- ½ teaspoon dried thyme
- ¼ teaspoon dried marjoram
- 4 cups vegetable broth, or store-bought, or water
- 1 cup plain unsweetened soy milk
- Salt and freshly ground black pepper
- 1 tablespoon minced fresh parsley, garnish

Directions:

1. In a large saucepan, heat the oil over medium heat. Add the shallots, carrots, parsnips, potatoes and garlic. Cover and cook until softened for about 5 minutes. Add the thyme, marjoram and broth and bring to a boil. Reduce the heat to low and simmer, uncovered, until the vegetables are tender for about 30 minutes.

2. Finish and serve

3. If necessary, pour the soup into the pot with an immersion blender or food processor, then return it to the pot. Stir in the soy milk and taste, adjusting the seasoning if necessary. Heat the soup over low heat until hot. Pour into bowls, sprinkle with parsley, then serve.

Chickpea and Sweet Potato Stew

Prep Time: 5 min   **Cooking Time:** 35 min   **Servings:** 4

Ingredients:

- 14 ounces cooked chickpeas
- 1 small sweet potato, peeled, cut into ½-inch cubes
- 1 medium red onion, sliced
- 3 ounces baby spinach
- 14 ounces crushed tomatoes
- 2 teaspoons minced garlic
- 1 teaspoon salt
- 1 1/2 teaspoons ground cumin
- 2 teaspoons harissa paste
- 2 teaspoons maple syrup
- ½ teaspoon ground black pepper
- 2 teaspoons sugar
- 1 tablespoon olive oil
- 1/2 cup vegetable stock
- 2 tablespoons chopped parsley
- 1 ounce slivered almonds, toasted
- Brown rice, cooked, for serving

Directions:

1. Take a large saucepan, put it on low heat, add the oil and when it is hot, add the onion and garlic and cook for 5 minutes.

2. Then add the sweet potatoes, drizzle with cumin, stir in the harissa paste and cook for 2 minutes until roasted.

3. Bring the heat to medium-low, add the tomatoes and chickpeas, pour in the vegetable broth, stir in the maple syrup and sugar and simmer for 25 minutes until the potatoes have softened, stirring every 10 minutes.

4. Then add the spinach, cook for 1 minute until the leaves are wilted and season with salt and black pepper.

5. When finished, distribute the cooked rice between the bowls, garnish with the stew, garnish with parsley and almonds and serve.

Nutrition:

Calories: 348 Cal Fat: 16.5 g Carbs: 41.2 g Protein: 7.2 g Fiber: 5.3 g

Almond Soup With Cardamom

Prep Time: 5 min   **Cooking Time:** 35 min   **Servings:** 4

Ingredients:

- 1 tablespoon extra-virgin olive oil
- 1 medium onion, chopped
- 1 medium russet potato, chopped
- 1 medium red bell pepper, chopped
- 4 cups vegetable broth, homemade or water
- ½ teaspoon ground cardamom
- Salt and freshly ground black pepper
- ½ cup almond butter
- ¼ cup sliced toasted almonds, for garnish

Directions:

1. In a large saucepan, heat the oil over medium heat. Add the onion, potato and pepper. Cover and cook until softened for about 5 minutes. Add the broth, cardamom and salt and pepper to taste. Bring to a boil, then lower the heat to low and simmer, uncovered, until the vegetables are tender for about 30 minutes.

2. Add the almond butter and season in the pot with an immersion blender or food processor, little by little if necessary, then return to the pot.

3. Finish and serve

4. Heat over medium heat until hot. Taste and adjust toppings as needed, then add more broth or soy milk as needed to achieve desired consistency.

5. Pour the soup into bowls, sprinkle with sliced toasted almonds, then serve.

Artichoke Soup

Prep Time: 10 min   **Cooking Time:** 20 min   **Servings:** 4

Ingredients:

- 1 tablespoon extra-virgin olive oil
- 2 medium shallots, chopped
- 2 (10-ounce) packages frozen artichoke hearts, thawed
- 3 cups vegetable broth, homemade or water
- 1 teaspoon fresh lemon juice
- Salt
- 1/3 cup almond butter
- ⅛ teaspoon ground cayenne
- 1 cup plain unsweetened soy milk
- 1 tablespoon snipped fresh chives, for garnish
- 2 tablespoons sliced toasted almonds, for garnish

Directions:

1. In a large saucepan, heat the oil over medium heat. Add the shallots, cover and cook until softened. Uncover and mix in the artichoke hearts, broth, lemon juice and salt. Bring to a boil, then lower the heat and simmer, uncovered, until the artichokes are tender for about 20 minutes.

2. Add the almond butter and cayenne pepper to the artichoke mixture.

3. Finish and serve

4. Blend in a high-speed blender or food processor, in batches if needed, then return to the pot. Stir in the soy milk, taste and adjust toppings as needed. Boil the soup over medium heat until hot.

5. Pour into bowls, sprinkle with chives and almonds, then serve.

Rice-Pea Soup

Prep Time: 5 min   **Cooking Time:** 45 min   **Servings:** 4

Ingredients:

- 2 tablespoons extra-virgin olive oil
- 1 medium onion, minced
- 2 garlic cloves minced
- 1 cup Arborio rice
- 6 cups vegetable broth or water
- Salt and freshly ground black pepper
- 1 (16-ounce) bag frozen petite green peas
- ¼ cup chopped fresh flat-leaf parsley

Directions:

1. In a large saucepan, heat the oil over medium heat. Add the onion and garlic, cover and cook until softened for about 5 minutes.

2. Uncover and add the rice, broth, salt and pepper. Bring to a boil, then reduce the heat to low. Cover and simmer until the rice begins to soften for about 30 minutes.

3. Finish and serve

4. Stir in the peas and cook, uncovered, for 15-20 minutes. Add the parsley and serve

Mushroom Stew

Prep Time: 10 min   **Cooking Time:** 50 min   **Servings:** 6

Ingredients:

- 1 to 2 teaspoons extra-virgin olive oil
- 2 cups chopped mushrooms
- ½ to 1 teaspoon salt
- 1 onion, chopped, or 1 teaspoon onion powder
- 3 or 4 garlic cloves, minced, or ½ teaspoon garlic powder
- 1 tablespoon dried herbs
- ¾ cup brown rice
- ¼ cup wild rice or additional brown rice
- 3 cups water
- 3 cups Vegetable Broth or store-bought broth
- 2 to 4 tablespoons balsamic vinegar (optional)
- Freshly ground black pepper
- 1 cup frozen peas, thawed
- 1 cup unsweetened nondairy milk (optional)
- 1 to 2 cups chopped greens, such as spinach, kale, or chard

Directions:

1. Heat the olive oil in a large saucepan over medium-high heat.

2. Add the mushrooms and a pinch of salt and sauté for about 4 minutes, until the mushrooms have softened. Add the onion and garlic (if using fresh) and sauté for another 1 or 2 minutes. Stir in the dried herbs (plus onion powder and / or garlic powder, if using), white or brown rice, wild rice, water, vegetable broth, vinegar (if using) and salt and pepper to taste. Bring to a boil, lower the heat and cover the pot. Boil the soup for 15 minutes (for white rice) or 45 minutes (for brown rice).

3. Finish and serve

4. Turn off the heat and stir in the peas, milk (if used) and vegetables. Let the vegetables dry before serving.

5. Leftovers can be stored in an airtight container for up to 1 week in the refrigerator or up to 1 month in the freezer.

Per Serving (2 cups):

Calories: 201; Protein: 6g; Total fat: 3g; Saturated fat: 0g; Carbohydrates: 44g; Fiber: 4g

Butternut & Lentil Soup

Prep Time: 5 min   **Cooking Time:** 55 min   **Servings:** 4

Ingredients:

- 1 tablespoon extra-virgin olive oil
- 1 medium onion, chopped
- 1 medium butternut squash, peeled and diced
- 1 garlic clove, minced
- 1 tablespoon minced fresh ginger
- 1 tablespoon hot or mild curry powder
- 1 (14.5-ounce) can crushed tomatoes
- 1 cup red lentils, picked over, rinsed, and drained
- 5 cups vegetable broth, homemade (see Light Vegetable Broth) or store-bought, or water
- Salt and freshly ground black pepper
- 3 cups chopped stemmed Swiss chard

Directions:

1. In a large saucepan, heat the oil over medium heat. Add the onion, pumpkin and garlic. Cover and cook until softened for about 10 minutes.

2. Mix the ginger and curry powder, then add the tomatoes, lentils, broth, salt and pepper. Bring to a boil, then lower the heat to low and simmer, uncovered, until the lentils and vegetables are tender. Stir occasionally for about 45 minutes.

3. Finish and serve

4. About 15 minutes before serving, stir in the chard. Taste and adjust toppings as needed, then serve.

Spinach, Walnut, & Apple Soup

Prep Time: 10 min   **Cooking Time:** 20 min   **Servings:** 4

Ingredients:

- 1 tablespoon extra-virgin olive oil
- 1 small onion, chopped
- 3 cups vegetable broth, homemade or store-bought, or water
- 2 Fuji or other flavorful apples
- 1 cup apple juice
- 4 cups fresh spinach
- ¾ cup ground walnuts
- 1 teaspoon minced fresh sage or ½teaspoon dried
- ¼ teaspoon ground allspice
- Salt and freshly ground black pepper
- 1 cup soy milk
- ¼ cup toasted walnut pieces

Directions:

1. In a large saucepan, heat the oil over medium heat. Add the onion, cover and cook until softened for 5 minutes. Add about 1 cup of vegetable stock, cover and cook until onion is very soft for another 5 minutes.

2. Peel, core and chop one of the apples, then add it to the pot with the onion and stock. Add the apple juice, spinach, chopped walnuts, sage, allspice, with the remaining 2 cups of broth, salt and pepper. Bring to a boil, then reduce the heat to low and simmer for 10 minutes.

3. Place the soup in the pot with an immersion blender or food processor, in batches if necessary, and return it to the pot. Stir in the soy milk and heat over medium heat until hot.

4. Finish and serve

5. Chop the remaining apple. Pour the soup into the bowls, garnish each bowl with some chopped apple, sprinkle with the walnut pieces, then serve.

Soup With Pecans & Ginger

Prep Time: 10 min   **Cooking Time:** 30 min   **Servings:** 4

Ingredients:

- 1/3 cup toasted pecans
- 2 tablespoons chopped crystallized ginger
- 1 tablespoon canola or grapeseed oil
- 1 medium onion, chopped
- 1 celery rib, chopped
- 1 teaspoon grated fresh ginger
- 5 cups vegetable broth, homemade or store-bought, or water
- 1 kabocha squash, peeled, seeded, and cut into ½-inch dice
- ¼ cup pure maple syrup
- 2 tablespoons soy sauce
- ¼ teaspoon ground allspice
- Salt and freshly ground black pepper
- 1 cup plain unsweetened soy milk

Directions:

1. In a food processor, combine the pecans and crystallized ginger and press until coarsely chop. To put aside.

2. In a large saucepan, heat the oil over medium heat. Add the onion, celery and fresh ginger. Cover and cook until softened for about 5 minutes. Mix the broth and pumpkin, cover and bring to a boil. Lower the heat to low and simmer, covered, stirring occasionally until the squash is tender for about 30 minutes.

3. Stir in the maple syrup, soy sauce, allspice, salt and pepper. Pu r é e into the pot with an immersion blender or food processor, in batches if necessary, and return to the pot.

4. Finish and serve

5. Stir in the soy milk and heat over low heat until hot. Pour the soup into bowls and sprinkle the pecan and ginger mixture, then serve.

Thai Soup

Prep Time: 5 min   **Cooking Time:** 25 min   **Servings:** 4

Ingredients:

- 1 tablespoon canola or grapeseed oil
- 1 medium onion, chopped
- 2 tablespoons minced fresh ginger
- 2 tablespoons soy sauce
- 1 tablespoon light brown sugar (optional)
- 1 teaspoon Asian chili paste
- 2½ cups light vegetable broth or water
- 8 ounces extra-firm tofu, drained and cut into ½-inch dice
- 2 (13.5-ounce) cans unsweetened coconut milk
- 1 tablespoon fresh lime juice
- 3 tablespoons chopped fresh cilantro, for garnish

Directions:

1. In a large saucepan, heat the oil over medium heat. Add the onion and ginger and cook until softened for about 5 minutes. Incorporate the soy sauce, sugar and chili paste. Add the broth and bring to a boil. Reduce heat to medium and simmer for 15 minutes.

2. Strain the broth and discard the solids. Return the broth to the pot over medium heat. Add the tofu and mix in the coconut milk and lime juice. Simmer for 5 more minutes to allow the flavors to blend.

3. Finish and serve

4. Pour into bowls, sprinkle with cilantro, then serve.

Thai Coconut Soup

Prep Time: 10 min   **Cooking Time:** 15 min   **Servings:** 12

Ingredients:

- 2 mangos, peeled, cut into bite-size pieces
- 1/2 cup green lentils, cooked
- 2 sweet potatoes, peeled, cubed
- 1/2 cup quinoa, cooked
- 1 green bell pepper, cored, cut into strips
- ½ teaspoon chopped basil
- ½ teaspoon chopped rosemary
- 2 tablespoons red curry paste
- 1/4 cup mixed nut
- 2 teaspoons orange zest
- 30 ounces coconut milk, unsweetened

Directions:

1. Take a large saucepan, put it on medium-high heat, add the sweet potatoes, pour in the milk and bring the mixture to a boil.

2. Then bring the heat to medium-low, add the remaining shopping list: except quinoa and lentils, stir and cook for 15 minutes until the vegetables are soft.

3. Then stir in the quinoa and lentils, cook for 3 minutes until hot, then serve.

Nutrition:
Calories: 232 Cal Fat: 19.8 g Carbs: 10.2 g Protein: 7.8 g Fiber: 0.8 g

Easy Corn Chowder

Prep Time: 15 min   **Cooking Time:** 15 min   **Servings:** 4

Ingredients:

- 2 tablespoons olive oil or other vegetable oil, such as coconut oil
- 1 onion, chopped
- 1 cup chopped fennel bulb or celery
- 2 carrots, peeled and chopped
- 1 red bell pepper, finely chopped
- ¼ cup all-purpose flour
- 6 cups vegetable stock
- 2 cups fresh or canned corn
- 2 cups cubed red potato
- 1 cup unsweetened almond milk or other unsweetened nut or grain milk
- ½ teaspoon sriracha sauce or chili paste (optional)
- sea salt
- freshly ground black pepper

Directions:

1. In a large saucepan, heat the olive oil over medium-high heat until it glows.

2. Add the onion, fennel, carrots and bell pepper and cook, stirring occasionally, until the vegetables soften, about 3 minutes.

3. Sprinkle the flour over the vegetables and continue to cook, stirring constantly, for about 2 minutes.

4. Incorporate the vegetable broth, using a spoon to scrape any bits of flour or vegetables from the bottom of the pan. Keep stirring until the liquid comes to a boil and the soup begins to thicken. Turn the heat down to medium heat.

5. Finish and serve

6. Add corn, potatoes, almond milk, and Sriracha, if using. Simmer until potatoes are soft, about 10 minutes. Season with salt and pepper. Serve hot.

Vegetable Bisque

Prep Time: 10 min   **Cooking Time:** 15 min   **Servings:** 6

Ingredients:

- 1 large onion, coarsely chopped
- 2 medium carrots, coarsely chopped
- 1 large russet potato, peeled and cut into ½-inch dice
- 1 medium zucchini, thinly sliced
- 1 large ripe tomato, quartered
- 2 garlic cloves, crushed
- 2 tablespoons extra-virgin olive oil
- ½ teaspoon dried savory
- ½ teaspoon dried thyme
- Salt and freshly ground black pepper
- 4 cups vegetable broth, homemade or store-bought, or water
- 1 tablespoon minced fresh parsley, for garnish

Directions:

1. Preheat the oven to 400 ° F. In a lightly oiled 9 x 13-inch pan, place the onion, carrots, potatoes, zucchini, tomato, and garlic. Season with oil and season with savory, thyme, salt and pepper to taste.

2. Bake

3. Cover tightly with foil and cook until softened for about 30 minutes. Uncover and bake, stirring once until the vegetables are lightly browned.

4. Finish and serve

5. Transfer the roasted vegetables to a large pot, add the broth and bring to a boil. Lower the heat and simmer, uncovered, for 15 minutes.

6. Place the soup in the pot with an immersion blender or food processor, in batches if necessary, then return it to the pot. Heat over medium heat until hot. Taste, adjusting toppings if necessary.

7. Pour into bowls, sprinkle with parsley, then serve

Pomegranate and Walnut Stew

Prep Time: 10 min   **Cooking Time:** 55 min   **Servings:** 6

Ingredients:

- 1 head of cauliflower, cut into florets
- 1 medium white onion, peeled, diced
- 1 1/2 cups California walnuts, toasted
- 1 cup yellow split peas
- 1 1/2 tablespoons honey
- ¼ teaspoon salt
- ½ teaspoon turmeric
- ½ teaspoon cinnamon
- 2 tablespoons olive oil, separated
- 4 cups pomegranate juice
- 2 tablespoons chopped parsley
- 2 tablespoons chopped walnuts, for garnishing

Directions:

1. Take a medium skillet, put it on medium heat, add the walnuts, cook for 5 minutes until roasted and then let it cool for 5 minutes.

2. Transfer the nuts to the food processor, blend for 2 minutes until ground and set aside until needed.

3. Take a large pan, put it on medium heat, add 1 tablespoon of oil and when it is hot, add the onion and cook for 5 minutes until soft.

4. Switch the heat to medium-low heat, then add the lentils and walnuts, stir in the cinnamon, salt and turmeric, pour in the honey and pomegranate, stir until blended and simmer for 40 minutes until the sauce has reduced by half and the lentils have softened.

5. Meanwhile, place the cauliflower florets in a food processor and then blend for 2 minutes until the mixture resembles rice.

6. Take a medium frying pan, put it on medium heat, add the remaining oil and when it is hot, add the rice to the cauliflower, cook for 5 minutes until softened, then season with salt.

7. Serve the cooked pomegranate and walnut sauce with cooked cauliflower rice and garnish with walnuts and parsley.

Nutrition:

Calories: 439 Cal Fat: 25 g Carbs: 67 g Protein: 21 g Fiber: 3 g

Lentil & Chickpea Stew

Prep Time: 5 min   **Cooking Time:** 55 min   **Servings:** 4

Ingredients:

- ¾ cup brown lentils, picked over, rinsed, and drained
- 2 tablespoons extra-virgin olive oil
- ½cup chopped green onions
- 2 teaspoons minced fresh ginger
- ¾ cup long-grain brown rice
- ½ cup dried apricots, quartered
- ¼ cup golden raisins
- ¼ teaspoon ground allspice
- ¼ teaspoon ground cumin
- ¼ teaspoon ground cayenne
- 1 teaspoon turmeric
- Salt and freshly ground black pepper
- 1/3 cup pomegranate molasses, homemade or store-bought
- 3 cups water
- 1½ cups cooked or 1 (15.5-ounce) can chickpeas, drained and rinsed
- ¼ cup minced fresh cilantro or parsley

Directions:

1. Soak the lentils in a medium bowl of hot water for 45 minutes. Drain and set aside.

2. In a large saucepan, heat the oil over medium heat. Add the green onions, ginger, soaked lentils, rice, apricots, raisins, allspice, cumin, cayenne, turmeric, salt and pepper. Cook and mix for 1 minute.

3. Add the pomegranate molasses and water, then bring to a boil. Reduce the heat to a minimum. Cover and simmer until the lentils and rice are tender for about 40 minutes.

4. Finish and serve

5. Incorporate the chickpeas and coriander. Simmer, uncovered, for 15 minutes to reheat and let the flavors blend. Serve immediately

Sweet Potato, Kale and Peanut Stew

Prep Time: 10 min   **Cooking Time:** 45 min   **Servings:** 3

Ingredients:

- 1/4 cup red lentils
- 2 medium sweet potatoes, peeled, cubed
- 1 medium white onion, peeled, diced
- 1 cup kale, chopped
- 2 tomatoes, diced
- 1/4 cup chopped green onion
- 1 teaspoon minced garlic
- 1 inch of ginger, grated
- 2 tablespoons toasted peanuts
- ¼ teaspoon ground black pepper
- 1 teaspoon ground cumin
- 1/2 teaspoon turmeric
- 1/8 teaspoon cayenne pepper
- 1 tablespoon peanut butter
- 1 1/2 cups vegetable broth
- 2 teaspoons coconut oil

Directions:

1. Take a medium saucepan, put it on medium heat, add the oil and when it melts add the onions and cook for 5 minutes.

2. Then stir in the ginger and garlic, cook for 2 minutes until fragrant, add the lentils and potatoes along with all the spices and mix until blended.

3. Stir in the tomatoes, pour in the broth, bring the mixture to a boil, then bring the heat to low and simmer for 30 minutes until cooked.

4. Then mix the peanut butter until incorporated and then blend using a hand blender until half pure.

5. Return the stew to low heat, stir in the kale, cook for 5 minutes until the leaves wilt, then season with black pepper and salt.

6. Garnish the stew with peanuts and green onions and serve.

Nutrition:

Calories: 401 Cal Fat: 6.7 g Carbs: 77.3 g Protein: 10.8 g Fiber: 16 g